AF589428

**POETRY**
by *leseliey rose*

**ART**
by *stephanie holloway*

for information contact hello@awakenlovethebook.com.

isbn 979-8-218-92666-3
www.awakenlovethebook.com

a message to
the LOVE in every heart

may it inspire hope, faith,
creativity, and courage.

within and without
timeless and everlasting
unique and universal
is the love of god

**CONTENTS**

ENCIRCLE ME ........ 1
WATER ........ 5
ROCK ........ 7
CLOUDS & STREAMS ........ 9
ZENITH ........ 11
MY BLOOD SINGS ........ 13
DESCENDANTS ........ 15
TIME ........ 19
LEAVES ........ 21
THE WISDOM OF OAK TREES ........ 22
RUSH ........ 23
WANT ........ 26
TRUTH ........ 27
LOVE LOVES ........ 29
INFINITE ........ 31

1

## ENCIRCLE ME

encircle me
in strong arms
like a bear hug
but not

let the circle
be snug
but not too tight
steady but secure

let me cry
like i'm not in my 40s
ugly cry existential tears
sob and shake
as i lament
the world
we've made

let me stay
as long as it takes
to feel soothed

whisper to me
that i'm safe and
tell me to give you
the weight off my shoulders

pat me on the bridge
called my back
like we pat
baby bottoms at bedtime

let me lay
my head on your chest
feel its rise and fall
hear your heart beat
and remember...

there's a god
that breathes us
that lives in us

and tell me
god is not done
with this world
not done
with me
yet

and let me
believe you

encircled
in strong arms
let me believe
it's all going to be okay

## WATER

warm and cloudy
with sustenance
for survival
waves carrying
sound and dreams
of gentle beginnings

we begin in water

*before you were born, i knew you...*

ocean, sea, sacred
the fusion of parts
bonded because
they know
we need each other
to survive

*just add water...*

to plant, to root, to grow
to cleanse, to restore, to thrive
full, abundant and free

we belong to
we live, move, and
have our being in water

the color of water
shows us
who we are

we begin
and end

*the substance of things hoped for...*

water

*i am inviting the solid outer ground to meet my strengthening inner grounds, from which everything i can offer the world flows.* - ruth allen

## ROCK

my seat meets
codified centuries gently

i sit on the edge
of the world
like a bird perched
on a cliff

i swing my legs
with the wind

a tsunami
carries my tears

through it i hum
new world songs
with lyrics in languages
yet unspoken

i hold heartbreak at bay
as humanity waivers
and wails and
leaders
lose their way

as long as
the earth
breathes
i know
magic lives
and
i believe
in redemption

## CLOUDS & STREAMS

there are those
who live
in a cloud
of nightmares
toiling in
smoke and mirrors
seeing by
their own sight

*mortals as they walk cannot direct their own steps*

and
there are those of us
who swim
in the slipstream
commended spirits
blinded
guided by
love's light

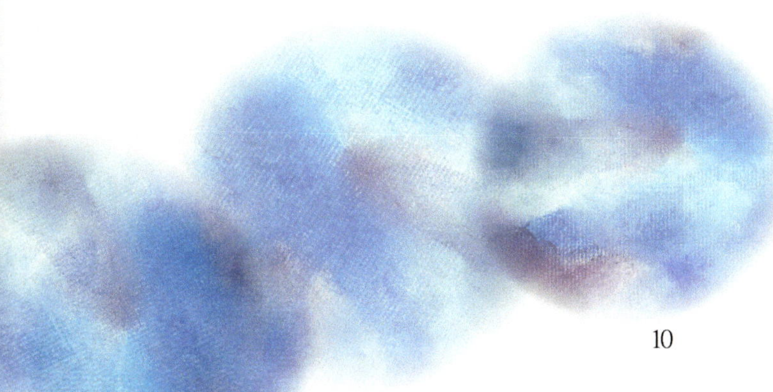

*there's nothing new under the sun, but there are new suns.*
-octavia butler

## ZENITH

my pace is
belly fire pace
like baldwin

my intention
consecrated
like rosa's resolve

my persistence
holy conviction
like king

my capacity
miraculous
like harriet's vision

my courage
purposeful and planned
comes from beyond

before i was born
god set me apart
because she knew
*greater works than these*
i would do

i am beyond
my blue hour
i am a new sun

## MY BLOOD SINGS

my blood flows
fierce and fiery
and faith-filled

it flows thick
with wisdom
of worlds
far and wide
real  imagined
now and then
before  after
in between
and yet to come

it sings to me
as it dances
in my veins

*we are rock and water*
*earth and wind*
*east born rising*
*west set resting*
*ever breathing*
*ever creating*
*ever singing*

*we are here*
*we see you*
*we know you*
*we dreamed you*

*we promised you*

## DESCENDANTS

today we reap
the harvest of yesterday's
tainted soils –
blood. hate. willful blindness.

rains rush in
to reveal the holes
in the roof
of the house
capitalism and supremacy built.

winds rip away
illusions of all right
lift up the absurdity
of *that's just the way it is* thinking
of individualistic
as any way to be.

*let your heart take courage.*

resist, open, and see...

resist the urge
to plug and patch
and catch
rain to water
the same gnarly soil
surrounding a sordid house.

open the doors, the windows,
the basement, the cellar,
the attic, the bowels
break open
your heart
and let rain
wash you free.

see me in your soul
look behind and beyond
cloudy eyes
the light is coming
the promise of a new harvest
the making of a new house.

*we can always be made new.*

be new and believe...

be new and build
dream and create
like my first breath
depends on you

plant mustard seeds
in fresh earth
like my life and the lives of
my children's children matter.

believe you are
*the way, the truth and the light.*

they say: *wisdom often*
*gathers in low places...*

build a bridge
from the inside out
from your nightmares undone
to your grandest dreams
for me
for us
for them.

*we are meant to survive.*

i will exist
because
you resist
you open
you see
you become
you believe
and
you build.

*blessed are those who*
*believe without seeing.*
you are the architects
of generations of tomorrows...

give up and i die
they die
we die
again and again.
love and i live.

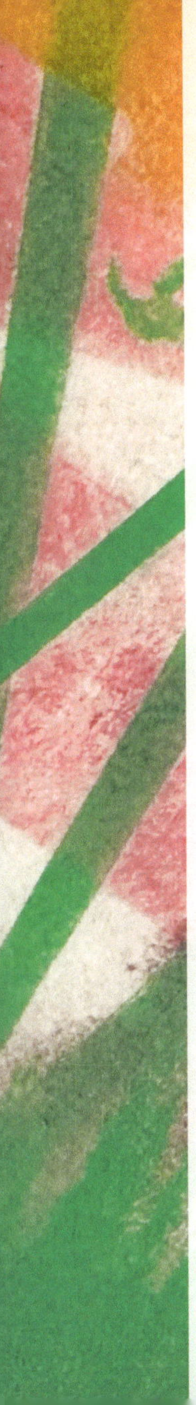

love a redemptive,
unwavering love
and i live
they live
we live.

## TIME

at the beginning
of what never began

i was sacred
celestial, ceremonial
rooted in nature
sun, moon, stars and wind

i was witnessed
in season
seed, seedling,
plant, flower

i was cyclical
sundials and
mooncycles
dancing light and
growing shadows

i was multidimensional
all at once
then, now
and yet to be

i was birth and death
honored
whole and
cherished

i was gifted
held gingerly
given wisely

i was enough

## LEAVES

the veil is thinner
in the majesty of fall
the leaves teach us
the beauty of dying

*under the earth, always,*
*they reach for each other.*
-adrienne maree brown

**THE WISDOM OF OAK TREES**

in the meadow
at the rising of the sun
warm and whole
will you reach for me?

in the surf
at the stirring of the sea
cold and salted
will you reach for me?

in the tornado
at the whirling
of wind and matter
lashed and worn

in the clouds
insight of infinite blue
inspired and free
will you reach for me?

## RUSH

i am a summer girl
longing for fall

not for its crisp cool air
i like a hot 75 in the shade
80 in the sun

not for the rainbows of leaves
i enjoy them
but not enough to hurry
the death of summer green

i prefer summer over fall
peonies over mums
juneeteenth over halloween
long days over long nights
sexy sandals over heavy boots
ever enduring sun over
encroaching moontime

i long for fall
not for the cozy smell
of pumpkin spice
i delight in the smell
of fresh mint
in summer cocktails

i love the beginning
and the end of summer
but not enough
to rush through
the in between

i am a summer girl
rushing summer
longing for fall
because
i long for you

## WANT

i want you
like cereal wants milk
peanut butter wants jelly
and rice wants gravy

i yearn for you
like clouds yearn for rainbows
autumn leaves yearn to fall
and scorching grass yearns for rain

i dream of you
like toddlers dream of puppies
athletes dream of winning
and abolitionist dream of freedom

## TRUTH

i betray myself
everyday
i'm not
loving you

## LOVE LOVES

love loves without fear
  of rejection, betrayal, or abandonment
without resentment
  harbored from days when
  we were not our best selves
without jealousy
  of talent, accomplishment, or accolades
love loves freely
  with faithful abandon
abundantly
  derived and flowing from infinite supply
love loves strong
  with conviction in turbulent times
passionately
  with intensity, eros, pleasure
love loves easy
  as tangible as air
  as natural as breath
love loves.

LOVE
LOVE
LOVE

## INFINITE

i love you
with an
inexhaustible love
honored
to witness
your majesty
and might
grateful
to bask
in your
light

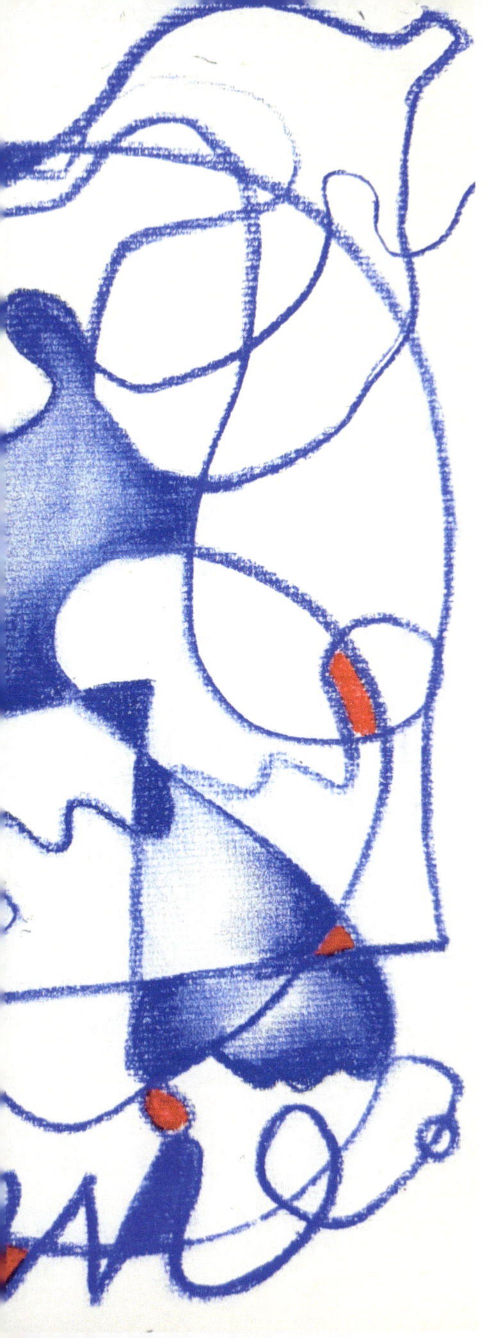

we are
all LOVE
learning
to remember.

www.ingramcontent.com/pod-product-compliance
Ingram Content Group UK Ltd.
Pitfield, Milton Keynes, MK11 3LW, UK
UKHW060404300726
14090UKWH00006B/416

* 9 7 9 8 2 1 8 9 2 6 6 6 3 *